of the Tree

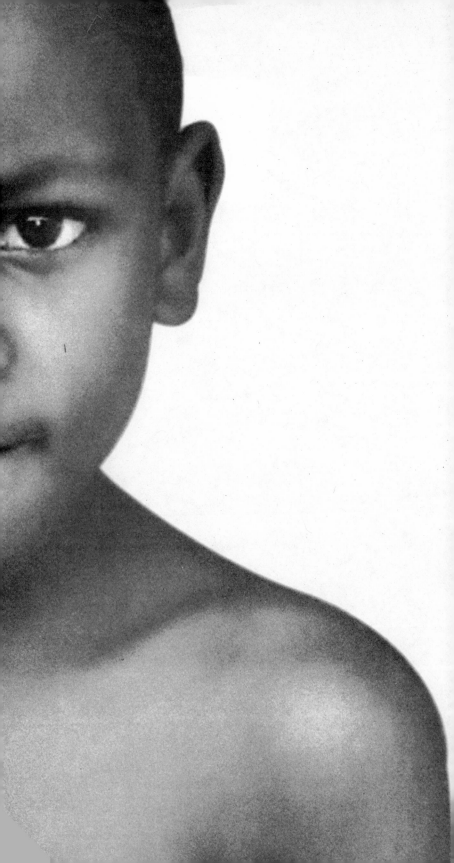

The Green Heart
of the Tree

Essays and Notes on a Time in Africa

A.S. Woudstra

The University *of* Alberta Press

Published by

The University of Alberta Press

Ring House 2

Edmonton, Alberta, Canada T6G 2E1

National Library of Canada Cataloguing in Publication

Woudstra, A. S. (Annette Schouten), 1975–

   The green heart of the tree : essays and notes on a time in Africa /

   A.S. Woudstra.

(cuRRents)

Includes index.

ISBN-13: 978-0-88864-476-3

   1. Woudstra, A .S. (Annette Schouten), 1975– —Travel—Africa. 2. Africa—
Description and travel. I. Title. II. Series: Currents (Edmonton, Alta.)

PS8645.O92G74 2007   916.72104'42   C2006-906858-5

Some of essays in this volume have appeared elsewhere: *Other Voices* ("Swallow
the Black Seeds"); *Queen's Quarterly* ("A Necessary Silence" and "Fish and Fetish");
Brick, A Literary Journal ("A Deepening Circle" and "The Green Heart of the Tree").

First edition, first printing, 2007

All rights reserved.

Printed and bound in Canada by Marquis Book Printing Inc., Montmagny, Quebec.

A volume in (cuRRents), a Canadian literature series.

Jonathan Hart, series editor

The University of Alberta Press is committed to protecting our natural environment.
As part of our efforts, this book is printed on Enviro Paper: it contains 100% post-
consumer recycled fibres and is acid- and chlorine-free.

The University of Alberta Press gratefully acknowledges the support received for
its publishing program from The Canada Council for the Arts. The University of
Alberta Press also gratefully acknowledges the financial support of the Government
of Canada through the Book Publishing Industry Development Program (BPIDP)
and from the Alberta Foundation for the Arts for its publishing activities.

 Canada Council
for the Arts   Conseil des Arts
du Canada   Canadä

for Doug and Susanna

and for Shawna

Contents

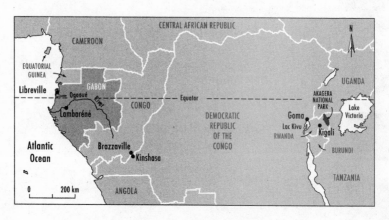

MAP AREA

Foreword

In the first days of 2002 I left Canada with my husband and three-year-old daughter for a new, indefinite home in Africa. We had done a lot of travelling before this, but had never visited the African continent. And this was not a trip: it was emigration, a true voyage out. Our first set of tickets took us to Kigali, Rwanda, where for several months we lived in the garden guesthouse of a Belgian architect and his Rwandese wife. There we worked on our French language skills and my husband, Doug, worked at and studied a community health-care project that was similar to the one he would be running at our final destination of the central African country of Gabon.

Before we left we sold our house and nearly everything in it. We packed and sent four Rubbermaid containers on a ship to Libreville, the port and capital city of Gabon. One container was taken up almost entirely by our daughter Susanna's little red bike. Another held things like a printer and inks and paper. Toys and art supplies and linens took up another box, but books filled the fourth container and every other available space. Many came carry-on as well, and each trip back to Libreville from Canada brought more. Books have always been, for me, very necessary (if very weighty) companions. My husband has very generously helped to haul them around many countries for me, many times.

The most important, the irreplaceable, and immediately essential books have had to come carry-on, and I think that one of these was, from the very beginning, Tim Lilburn's *Living in the World as if it were Home*, a collection of essays. I mention it because, in sitting down to write this foreword, I realize how much the reading of (and maybe believing in) that book informed the writing of this one. It was Lilburn's book that helped bring me over the bridge from poetry to the essays I've written here. More importantly though, he taught me (as Annie Dillard and Simone Weil in their own ways have also done) that to continually be at wonder in this world, to be asking how to be here was an acceptable, and maybe even an important, occupation. In his description of the contemplative stance, I found a kind of home to live in and write from while I was very much not-at-home.

How we came to be not-at-home in the middle of the central African rainforest went something like this: My husband and I simply wanted to go. We wanted to work and learn new things in new places, we felt there might be something we could do or give, and we were tired of the getting-game. The North American habit of endless consumption had become—it seemed unavoidably—our own. We had lived here all of our lives. As soon as a rather obscure opportunity to leave came our way, we took it.

My husband, Doug, was a physical therapist at the time, and he was hired by a large European non-governmental organization (NGO) to be the director of a community-based rehabilitation project in Libreville. During the years we lived there, he trained the local staff, set up important connections to other philanthropic health-care providers in the country, and pressured the government to establish health-care policies that would give the poor better access to health-care services. He and his staff solved problems related to day-to-day health and rehabilitation in the poorest neighbourhoods of the city and surrounding villages, and worked to educate the community to respond to the needs of and advocate for its own members. We left when the local staff was ready and able to continue the work of the project on their own, which they continue to do today.

I went along for the ride. I read. I mothered our small daughter and tried to make a home in a foreign land for our family. I wrote—poetry at first—as I had been writing for several years before we moved abroad. But whether it was because I wasn't reading as much poetry (I was researching places and people) or because I had begun to feel the compact poems I was used to writing could no longer contain (much less name) the tumult in my head, within the first year of living in Gabon I had written my first essay, the one that follows: "The Green Heart of the Tree." I needed more room than a poem can provide, more pages to think through my new life and my new surroundings. The intimacy that is so necessary in poetry, I in my new land, utterly lacked.

I applied to a creative writing program that I could do through correspondence with a writer-mentor from Canada. I wrote, in my original proposal to the program, that I wanted to write essays that would "explore, in general, living in Africa—based on my own experiences, encounters, word of mouth, and pure speculation." Obviously I was keeping my options open. "I want to write with the attentive gaze of poetry—keeping a finger on the mysteries of things and of being, but also asking a good hard question or two. In tone I would like them to resemble meditations—a contemplative look at life and, perhaps, meaning." Perhaps. Meaning.

And in this proposal, at the beginning of the project that eventually became this book, I included a quotation from the Lilburn book that inspired and informed my own writing at that time: "Contemplative knowing...does not imagine that a thing known is one that rests easily in the palm of the mind, caught in description, known in its rough similarity to other things. Contemplation lets fall names, eschews power, to clear the ground for astonishment; it revels in eccentricity. It does not wish to subdue the world but to dwell in it."

That is what I wanted to do while I lived in Africa. I wanted not to name or subdue, but to dwell. In and with and on it all, I wanted to revel, as Lilburn said. I was astonished. Nothing could be truly known in the place I had landed to live in for a time. I wanted to write in a way that would somehow point in that direction. I hoped to be honest, to be clear and clean about what I was seeing and how I was feeling.

I won't pretend to have been or to be an excellent contemplative. But this kind of thinking about the new world around me, and an attempt to render this through the written word, was my intent. Contemplation offered me a way to recognize my longing to understand things and at the same time acknowledge the impossibility of that understanding. Where Lilburn looked, in his book, at the natural world in this way, I looked at the foreign places and people around me. I longed to be a part of it. I knew I could not be. So I tried to pay attention and I attempted to love it, to be in love with it, all.

But this kind of being in love and this way of writing isn't always easy or clear. Connections are not always possible to make. So what follows is not cohesive narrative nor is it a memoir. There are gaps and there are spaces around the words. (I'd like to think that there is room to breathe.) There is little mention of time, exact locations, or itineraries. Five journal entries are scattered throughout the book (all, mysteriously, regard various birds). These are, perhaps, more intimate views through the window of my study and into my then life.

I wrote all the essays in this collection at my bamboo desk in Libreville, Gabon, except for two. They are, I hope, and at best, meditations on various things. Turtle eggs in warm sand. Wild trees. Masked dancers. They are long and loving looks into mysterious life. If you feel a bit disoriented at times, that's exactly what I've hoped for.

These times are points on which a great many pressures bear down. The mind returns to them; their meaning is never resolved. They are doors banging on their hinges, disturbing the peace.

—ANNIE DILLARD, *In Transit*

The Green Heart of the Tree

I went walking clean and small down the white beach at low tide.
A cloudy afternoon in the dry season on the west coast of Africa, and
I was still new enough and Canadian enough to feel warm while the
Africans were wearing long sleeves and sweaters. I met no one on the
beach, and even the usual garbage must have gone back out with the
tide that morning—the sand was clear and smooth. The tropical trees
that lined the shore were dropping their massive seeds. I stopped at
a group of red rocks that sloped down the beach and into the sea. I
climbed onto the backs of a few low-lying clusters, and then I saw the
crabs.

Almost fifty of them; they were wet-black, slim-bodied, long-legged,
and fast. Each time I moved I sent more of them running to the far edge

of the rock where the waves hit and slopped over them. So I stopped and stood still where I could see them. They held on, unmoving when I was. I watched, getting wet from the spray, until I felt sorry for keeping them in suspense.

Walking the edge of the water back, a sudden fleet wave knocked me nearly over. I went home radiantly soggy.

We live close to the bones of life here, in heat and in blood. We live in the central African country of Gabon; the equator runs anonymous through the jungle just south of the capital, Libreville. A city wedged between the riotous green of the rainforest and the long-wandering sea. We've been here a while, but we won't stay forever.

My husband is with me, and my daughter who is four. She is in love with the teeming world and her backyard rope swing and the fact that it never will snow here. She keeps a sharp eye out for lizards and toads. My husband works in community health, he holds broken children and straightens twisted feet. I have a photograph of him under banana trees, inspecting a gunshot wound in the calf of a ten-year-old girl.

He comes home with dirt on the knees of his pants from the floors of the houses he works in, and I wash them out. And I write, trembling, gathering up the questions, and Africa asks many. The nights are dark, livid, long. I don't dream of answers—I just try to sleep.

How to live? The old question. Renewed for every person born and every person dying. Here, people ask it every day—in reverence and in fear—it is as relevant as bread to them. But it swallows us whole, we cannot manage it. Somehow all our lives it has been managed for us and made to lie quietly under beds and in dark corners. We look each other in the eye some nights and see only bewildered shadows. There are few words, and only small insights; we try instead to ask good questions. We cleave in attentive sorrow, just under the tough skin of life.

Our first months here fell in the heavy and hottest of seasons. On errands in town we would all sit in the front seat of the truck so our daughter could benefit from both the air-conditioning and the views. At a red light two boys ran up to our window, pressing their palms to the glass. They were badly burned, their faces warped, their hands missing fingers and curled protectively inward. One boy had no hand at all, just a smooth rounded stub at the end of one of his slim forearms.

We watched them, unable to move or to even think about what they wanted. When the light changed they ran to the sidewalk, and we drove away.

The child sitting beside me asks into the silence, "What happened to those kids?" and I try to give her a reasonable answer. She wants to know—will that happen to her, and I tell her no, it won't ever happen to her and so she forgets about it, relieved, facing forward to see whatever is coming up next.

What comes up next is always unknown. We don't belong here, we are nothing to Africa, we are homeless, we are odd. We rent a house with a large yard; it has three cool white bedrooms and a neat blue-tiled kitchen. A block away is the main road to town. Beside it, families live in wood shacks without doors and their children play in the dust kicked up by passing cars and trucks. In the rainy season, if it rains hard or long enough, sometimes a house there will be washed away, sometimes people drown. Or rainwater floods the latrines and the dirty water runs and then dries through the houses and people get sick. We live beside them, but the road we walk to meet is precarious and obscured.

The man who hemmed the curtains for my bedroom window lives there, a refugee from Guinea. And the man who fixed the air conditioning in the truck. I sat once in the tailor's only chair, my knees brushing against the bench where he worked. When he comes to my house with a delivery, he never forgets to ask how I am and how is my husband, and is the little girl well? He sends his generous greeting to them, which I usually remember to repeat. We try, we learn from each other, and sometimes we laugh—we are friendly, but are we friends? We shake hands easily enough but it is hard to hold on. If we held on, if we could, where would we go?

So many things divide us: education and landscape, history and language. Sometimes the space feels as impenetrable as the space that separates me from river, rock, and those black crabs.

Is it a useful question? I know it is more fashionable to talk about what pulls us together. But driving home I see a woman inches away from the road my truck is flying down and she crawls with her hands pushed into plastic sandals and dragging withered legs. She has a shanty so small I can't pick it out in the daylight but at night she somehow manages a huge smoking pot over an open fire. How can I pretend to imagine what her life has been like, or the feel of the fight she takes up every morning?

Maybe the way to be here is not in imagination but in work—pure and persistent. I have a feeling this is my husband's idea, but I know he carries with him the stories of the people he sees, regardless. He's making the plans for a little wooden chair for children with cerebral palsy so they can sit up and see the faces of their brothers, or watch their sisters dance. He visits a baby girl who sits unmoving on the floor, often alone in a windowless room. Once she sat watching him, sucking on a small chicken bone. He met a boy who went to school one day and came home mysteriously unable to walk. He won't go to school anymore, slumped in the heat and the pain of his body. He's been given a wheelchair but scooting around on the ground is faster so his legs are covered in open, dirty sores. If these get infected and remain untreated, the infection might travel into his bones and he'll need his legs amputated. Or maybe he will die. He is eight years old, but he will be dead long before there is someone who can say why.

How do we live our lives then, while we have them? On weekends we bring our questions to the sea's side and we look over the waves toward home. We learn the names of birds who arrive on resplendent wing, and we watch the orange heads of lizards nodding on top of the walls that surround our yard. We live, we live, this is what the banana tree says, growing out of the garbage heap at the edge of our street. And so say the children minding cattle high in the hills alone. We live with the dark seed of mystery, our lives, in the middle of general confusion. We live equally out of the garbage heap or the cultivated soil, and who is to say who bears better fruit? The force that moves in the green heart of the tree is carried in each, the designs for growth and fecundity, heedless and wild. We live, we shake briefly the hands of those with us, we carry our seeds, and we hope to stay on the rocks when the water hits hardest.

Down the road that passes our house and after a hill, a path splits off and runs through a village to a river. Someone mentioned this to us once, and the idea of a river running hidden through the bush next to our neighbourhood intrigued us. So one empty Saturday morning we decided to fill the day by looking for it.

We drove, tilting down the rutted path and slowly proceeding past shanties haphazardly built beside it. We drove blindly until the trail trickled into grasses far taller than the truck. Turning back, we spotted children down another skinny branch of the path, running half-hidden into an overgrown field. Four small boys and a wheelbarrow on some unfathomable errand. We waved them over and they came, very wary and serious. We asked them where the river was and they pointed silently, finally admitting that it was close, just there. Thanking them, we started in that direction but they waved us back and asked for a ride in the back of the truck. Then, smiling widely, they jumped in and stood legs wide apart and bellies pushed out, small faces into the wind.

We found it—the river—and it was not that far. We three got out and watched its vast coursing through banks spilled over with vine and the tree-giants leaning to water. The river exhaled a thick breath, fast and muddy. The boys watched us watching. Our daughter was bored; she wanted to get back in the truck. My husband asked the boys if they fished and they said they did—their father's canoe was just a short walk away—did we want it? We didn't want it. The boys shrugged.

What were we doing then looking at the river? What did we want? We had no real idea of where we were, or even what river we had found. So we returned the same way we came, with the boys in the back of the truck. They knocked on the roof of the cab when we reached their wheelbarrow and we let them off in the grass.

When they disappeared again we went back the only way we knew— down deep-pitted roads through the village, no names for the journey or for home.

The Volcano

Mount Nyiragongo, just outside the Congolese town of Goma, erupted on January 17, 2002, and sent all the nearby hills of Rwanda shuddering. We were less than two hundred kilometres away, in Kigali, and still just learning how to navigate the African roads when they began to buckle beneath us.

We had arrived in Kigali, the Rwandan capital, in the first week of January 2002: my husband, my three-year-old daughter, and I. "Baptized by fire," our regional director pronounced over us when we first met him, after he flew into Kigali to help with the trip we would be making to Goma as soon as we could.

We went to Goma to survey the damage done to a number of hospitals and health centres that the non-governmental organization (NGO) we worked for had lost in the lava flow, and we brought the first truck-load of medical supplies to the area. Three hundred thousand people had fled the eruption, east into neighbouring Rwandan towns and west into the Democratic Republic of Congo. They lined the roads out of and around the town, the only signs of life. Women, in their colourful wrap-around skirts, were the bright flags flying along the fringes of a desolate world.

The landscape was lunar—black, grey, pitted—and it was smoth-ered, utterly subdued. Only sometimes a carbonized tree still stood in the middle of the lava path, as though marking the spot of a particular death. The lava had cut the town in two. The day we arrived, only three days after the eruption, was the first day people were able to cross the lava path to the other side, and we joined the first crowds across. The land around us was frozen in a black boil, the lava heaped several feet deep in some spots, and smoking.

We climbed up onto the lava where it seemed a little narrower, where you could begin to see the other side, where the lava ended. But once we were on top of it, all that mattered was getting off again. The air above the lava trail was steaming, and the lava was still so hot in places that we had to skip or run over it, unable to take the time we needed to care-fully place our steps. It was treacherous work and we were enveloped in toxic-smelling haze. To find the hospital and health centre sites, we had to get across several long fingers of lava that flowed through the town. We took a lot of pictures, the first strange tourists to this unbe-lievable new world.

Few people died when Mount Nyiragongo erupted that day, though volcanoes have such deadly potential. I read up on them a little later. Volcanoes have killed tens of thousands of people in one literal blow. Major eruptions can change weather patterns around the world for years. But I also read about the life-giving capabilities of volcanoes and saw for myself that the soil in areas of volcanic activity is some of the most fertile in the world.

Looking back at my day on the volcano's path, I know I didn't think of any of its marvellous potential then. I only balked at the black waves that had swallowed the town. I thought I had seen hell, and that hell was irreversible. Inescapable, except for those of us who were Westerners, escape artists extraordinaire. We left with only the soles of our shoes slightly singed and a sulphurous smell in our hair. We were always able to slip out at the last moment, if we needed to. We left the Congolese and the Rwandans to their hell.

I'm not sure they saw it that way, though; they might have remembered what may come after the eruption; they seemed to be thinking about life. "Courage," our African colleagues said to one another as we viewed the devastation throughout the day, and to anyone who told us their story. Because they just got over it, literally. Three days later, the lava still creeping along in places, still hot, thousands of people just climbed right over it with their children on their backs, their sleeping mats on their heads, and their goats pulled behind them. They crossed over to find what was left, if anything, and to dig in again, as best they could.

Volcanoes live at the very edge of the known world; they are mysterious entrances to the centre of the earth. What lies beneath us is yet so unknown, and why and when it will sometimes explode is anyone's guess. To look into the vomited-out heart of a volcano is to look at a great mystery. The new/old earth we were standing on was shaken in those days after the eruption of Nyiragongo, and not for the last time.

I came across an article Annie Dillard wrote years ago, called "The Volcano." It's about writing.

"What is this writing life?" she asks. In answer she describes a day in which her typewriter erupts. "The old green Smith-Corona typewriter on the table was exploding with fire and ash.... Smoke and cinders poured out, noises exploded and spattered, black dense smoke rose up, and a wild deep fire lighted the whole thing. It shot sparks." The eruption lasts twenty minutes, though she hears occasional rumblings coming from it throughout the night. The next day she cleans it up, and that, it seems, is that. She writes, " I have had no trouble with it since. Of course, now I know it can happen."

We were lucky to be introduced to the "wild deep fire" that lights the whole thing, this world, nearly as soon as we had arrived in Africa. We knew then, right away, that it could happen, that anything could happen. We kept an eye out for shooting sparks. In an attempt to form an adequate response, I lighted a few fires of my own, I wrote it all down. Because, as Annie Dillard so vividly illustrates, writing can erupt with similar force.

These odd pieces I'm writing feel like eruptions to me, minor earthquakes still rumbling along the fault lines of lives and places. The mysterious origin is life: my life, as it was lived for a while in exile, in the stunning dis-connect from all that I knew or thought I knew, and all of the life and lives that I came across or that ran headlong into mine.

These essays are fragments. The truth of the whole might lie in the silences between them and in the spaces they contain. The stories in this book are bits of flaming rock, lofted from the smoking cauldrons of time and place, into my life. Now into yours.

A year after Mount Nyiragongo erupted, some colleagues visited us in our home in Gabon, after they had been to Goma. They told us that the lava still steamed when it rained. I read about this just recently, that lava is a poor heat conductor so it can smolder for decades, even centuries. It seems unbelievable to me. The lava stretching across Goma seemed so utterly dead, solid, immutable—yet somewhere it is sizzling still.

I wonder, and somehow I know, that these years in Africa will live on like that in me. Underground most of the time, memory seemingly gone cold, but remaining, impossibly, aflame.

How amazing that I have been set down here in this place. Right now there is birdsong—one song and then bits of chattering—and it is for me. Because I hear it, I am listening. The branch I can see out the window is moving, it has a new leaf, and another is dead, falling away. The clouds are wandering the sky, three egrets fly through the backyard. Ants are, as always, tramping out from under the windowsill and then down the wall to whatever it is that amuses them behind my filing cabinet. Now— thunder, a low growl. Diluted sunlight falls on the wooden head of a girl on my desk, burnishing a temple and an ear white with light.

I am in Africa. Does this matter? Life here is no more real than anywhere else, it is just that here we feel it. We feel the wind whipping past, we hear the strange voice around us. Meaning becomes lost just as often as it must anywhere else, but here we notice it. If we were not here, we would not be so simply alive. Pulled tight, ready to spring. Watching the world around us more carefully than we ever have, keening towards sorrow and beauty both.

2002

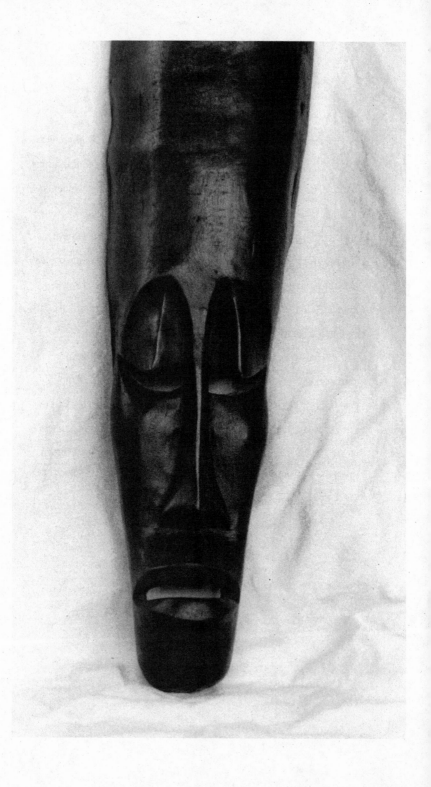

Swallow the Black Seeds

One winter we had three rooms on the side of a hill in Kigali. We abandoned one of them immediately—it was dark and smelled bad and you had to squeeze down narrow stairs and then through a skinny door to get into it. So we used only the main room with its large wooden table and slept all together in the other bedroom.

But we picked the wrong room: a few weeks after we arrived, it rained. The power went out, the thunder grumbled on all day, and my daughter kept pointing out that the rain here fell inside the house too. It came through the roof tiles into every room—except the one we had abandoned. We had to buy buckets from the Lebanese corner store to control the flooding. On sunny days my daughter used them outside on the terrace to swim in.

Rwanda—the first seeds of Africa planted into our lives and with it, hundreds of thousands of dead. Like the passion fruit we ate every day: black seeds swallowed down with the sweet sharp flesh and sown deep in our bodies. To eat a passion fruit, the dark dappled sphere of skin must be halved and the insides of the shells scraped clean. You swallow fruit, juice, and seeds—if you try to separate them in your mouth the seeds get caught and broken between teeth. Left behind are two deep bowls, emptied cups. A womb broken, wiped clean by a birth. Seeds like small ships carrying life mysterious within.

How to write Rwanda? The words I need are risky: genocide, mutilation, hatred, rape. Extermination. Words like knives that become either blunted or sharpened, depending on their use. Words that can wound: both those who hear them and those who write them. But better to use them and leave them out to be seen than left half-hidden, half-forgotten, waiting to be stumbled on or stolen away.

For a few months in the beginning of 2002 we lived in Kigali. My husband was in Rwanda to work for a community health project, to work with the living, so I took up with the dead. Rwanda was the ideal location, if there is such a thing, for thinking through death, and for beginning the work of love. Living in Rwanda, I struck up a friendship with the dead.

Gathering their stories, I longed to go blind. I resented the wholeness of my body, the seamless nature of my thinking. Beneath I could feel the holes, the frazzled edges of existence, the snapped thread of knowledge. The days there scratched; each morning I woke again raw. Keeping me company with the dead was my daughter. It was for her I kept buying little plastic bags of passion fruit, because they were her new favourite.

Fewer than ten years ago, in 1994, in a period of only about one hundred days, nearly a million people were brutally murdered here. Under eucalyptus and banana trees, on hills planted with tea and corn, in the deep ditches beside the dirt roads, in the small African country of Rwanda.

They were mostly cut to pieces with machetes. They were killed by neighbours and sometimes by relatives. Often the mayor or a priest organized rounding them up into hospitals or churches to be executed together in one horrific assault. Whole families were thrown into latrines. Infants and grandparents and pregnant women. Ten-year-old boys and favourite aunts. Philosophers, musicians, shoemakers, and farmers.

The United Nations had troops in Rwanda, and they knew what was happening. They had good opportunities to stop it, even before it really began, and they asked for permission to do so. The answer from head offices and powerful heads of state was essentially, no. The world watched. We watched, then walked away.

No one wears ribbons to remember Rwandans. From Africa now I watch the world launching into anti-terrorism campaigns and I wonder—where was all this compassionate zeal when it came to the massacre of hundreds of thousands of Africans? Where was the international coalition to bring to justice those responsible for the genocide here? Somehow the human misery and madness of the genocide has continued to be overlooked. Rwanda has been rejected by the world as being unworthy of communal grief.

There may be little point in writing or reading this essay. Because language, in the history of Rwanda, has demonstrated both its dangers and its powerlessness. Before the genocide in Rwanda had begun even to be envisioned, there were international conventions condemning such things. The Genocide Convention—signed by the very nations that a few decades later turned a blind eye to what they knew was happening in Rwanda—declares, essentially, that the international community has a moral responsibility to come to the aid of peoples who are threatened with elimination by others. This convention was signed in 1948, in the aftermath of World War II, in the hopes that something like the Nazi campaign against the Jews would never again be allowed to happen.

But all the declarations in the world were not enough to save a single Rwandan. In fact, the few UN soldiers who were allowed to stay in

Rwanda had their hands tied tightly by the words of their mandate. Only when the killing had stopped were they allowed to use them, and the weapons they carried: to kill the dogs eating the corpses of the people they had allowed to die.

In the face of such a story, what power is left in words?

But once you have made friends with the dead, you cannot leave them behind. Their stories follow me, I can't lose them. Here is one, and maybe one is enough: A woman went visiting a friend the day the Hutu Power groups began killing. While she was there, they came and killed everyone in the house. But this woman survived, though she watched her friend's family and her own being cut to pieces around her. Her husband found her the next day, bleeding from the places where they had cut off both her arms.

What I keep thinking of is the night she spent there, alone, alive. In the dark room of the dead.

To listen to someone is to put oneself in his place while he is speaking. To put oneself in the place of someone whose soul is corroded by affliction, or in near danger of it, is to annihilate oneself. It is more difficult than suicide would be for a happy child. Therefore the afflicted are not listened to. They are like someone whose tongue has been cut out and who occasionally forgets the fact. When they move their lips no ear perceives any sound. And they themselves soon sink into impotence in the use of language, because of the certainty of not being heard. [1]

— SIMONE WEIL

In Kigali I bought a mask. A long thin head of dark wood, the face carved into the bottom third. The forehead is vast and curves gently away from the wall it hangs on. The eyes are half closed, looking down under elongated lids. Its slender nose is pulled down by the mouth: an open, tongueless space that stretches across from both sides of the chin. It is the face of the afflicted.

Rwandans live like no other people on earth. Together they have killed and been killed, and now, together, they live. Their country is one of the most densely populated places on earth, and that is counting only the living. Think how many dead are still held by the living, in memory, in sight, in the spaces between every thought and each movement. When the worst of the genocide was finished, there were seven dead for each survivor. Seven silent voices for each one who speaks. Seven invisible for each person seen. The eyes of the living see through the dead, their feet crush the bones and the bodies and the blood.

Whatever the living do—both guilty and victim alike—is pressed down and held tight by fear and by sorrow. By violence let loose and allowed to rip lives apart. Life here is weighed down with grief and incredible fear. Who can live like this? Apparently, seven million Rwandans. I've seen them.

Where they live is incredibly beautiful, almost impossibly so. It is hard to reconcile the lush countryside with its recent history. The weather, when I lived there, was ideal, everything growing green and generous—birds singing. The only thing that kept me grounded was the dirt roads, which were in terrible shape and the colour of old blood.

Across from the little house we rented stood a huge shell of a devastated mansion. On the exposed third floor, the members of a large family were squatting, protected by an old green plastic UNHCR sheet. All around the broken house grew masses of corn. Between the corn and the deep ruts of the road stood teeming rows of enormous sunflowers, obscuring any possible path to the building. Once, when my daughter and I were admiring the flowers while we waited for a taxi, I spotted a woman standing there. She was watching us from deep within the shade of the sunflowers and corn. I was startled, but smiled, and then she turned and dissolved so silently, so completely, I was left wondering if I had only imagined her.

One evening not long after our arrival in Rwanda, we went out for dinner to the Mille Collines—the luxury hotel of Kigali. We were celebrating my husband's birthday and my own, both of which fell in the first month of our stay. In the bloodiest days of the genocide, scores of people fled here for protection and many of them were able, because of it, to stay alive. The manager distracted the would-be murderers, when they came to raid the hotel, with the vast quantities of alcohol he had on site.

The restaurant was on the third floor but was open to the night air and our table was right beside the balcony. If we leaned out from our seats we could see the pool glowing down in the grounds beneath us. There were four or five waiters per table, all in uniforms, all wearing white gloves. Geckos scaled the inside walls and as the evening grew darker, huge hairy moths began to fly inside the restaurant, catching the smaller insects that were circling the light fixtures above our heads. The moths were enormous and our daughter spent the rest of the night on my lap, keeping a wary eye on them until she fell into an exhausted sleep. That evening always stands out in my mind, eerily glowing as did the pool that night, a fragile island in the darkness, bright with some mysterious meaning, a message never quite revealed.

What if the seed within the passion fruit is not death, but truth, which is the same as love? Either way, it's all hard to swallow—perhaps it's an acquired taste. My daughter, though, would eat six of these fruit in one sitting, if I let her. To begin the work of love in the world is perhaps learning how to eat the passion fruit, developing the taste for the truth, no matter how tricky it is, or how bitter.

While we were in Kigali, a volcanic mountain erupted about three hundred kilometres away. At night we could feel the earth shake. But no one thought it odd enough to mention. Maybe Rwandans are already certain that they will not be heard. They have lost their voice with the dead around them.

If the suffering voice goes unheard in this world, then we must move with it beyond language. We must forget our own faces and wear wooden masks. Become friends with the dead. Learn to swallow the black seeds and cultivate a silence deep enough to make it possible to hear those who are speaking with tongues cut out.

The Elephant

But once, in Rwanda, we were taken high into the hills for honey.

We were living for a few months in Kigali when a friend and colleague offered to take us to the once popular Akagera Park for our first African safari. He warned us that he hadn't been there for years and he couldn't know what to expect. But we were eager to go, to get out of the city and the work we were doing, if just for a day. We were happy to be tourists for a while, a very odd thing to be, in Rwanda.

We left Kigali in the first light of the day, travelling in two trucks for safety. We stopped first at the abandoned hotel that once catered to safari-goers, years ago, before the genocide. During the worst days of the slaughter the staff fled the lodge that overlooks the grasslands and a lake. Packs of baboons lived there now and all sorts of other smaller monkeys, literally hanging around. I remember that nervous feeling you have in abandoned buildings mixed with the weird amusement of watching monkeys. And the ever-present chill of the past, inescapable in Rwanda, that makes you look into every roadside ditch for the bodies you half-expect are lying there, still. Beside the hotel, we looked into the crumbling swimming pool.

There were a lot of baboons, and baboons are terrible things, the way they show you their purple bottoms and then their large teeth. A pair began a spat while we were enjoying the view from the terraces behind the hotel, and we quickly left them to it.

At the building that marked the entrance to the unfenced park we picked up a young man who agreed to be our guide for the day. He was quite happy to see us, as we were the only visitors in the park that day. There was an old message board near the building and while we were waiting for the guide to get his things in order, our friend pointed it out while telling us about his visits here with his family when he was a child growing up in the Congo.

In those days, he told us, tacked onto this bulletin board was a warning to visitors not to leave their vehicles. A series of photos below the written warning illustrated the point. The photos had been taken by a man waiting in his vehicle for one of his fellow passengers who had ventured out to get a closer shot of a group of lions lazing around in the shade of a small clump of trees. One shot showed this man's back to the truck, crouched down and getting, presumably, the perfect shot. Beside it was a photo of what seemed to be the same scene, but with a lion in one corner of the frame, flying toward the figure of the crouching man. Then: the attack / the tearing apart of the photographer / the blood on the grass, on the lion's mouth.

Our friend described how shaken he had been, as a child, when he saw this series of photographs. We could see, while he told the story, how shaken he was still.

Soon we were on our way, down to the grasslands in the valley. Our Flemish friends had the guide and drove ahead of us; we followed in our own truck with a badly photocopied map. Akagera is enormous, covering 2,500 square kilometres—you could spend days here in the swamps, savannah, or hills. The wildlife population in the park had been decimated in the unstable years that surrounded the genocide, by poaching and then loss of land as the Rwandan government struggled to find space for the refugees returning after the war. It was, at one time, teeming with hippos and lions, antelope and thousands of birds. There are eight lakes in the park. We had our lunch beside one of them, inside a desolate gazebo, listening to the snorts of hippos hidden in the water. We followed few trails, instead ploughing our own way through valleys of long grasses where we trailed a group of giraffes. Up hills where we found herds of zebra. And in a forested area we drove aimlessly amid startled guinea fowl. Until we found the elephant.

I don't remember a thing about who found it or how. It was just somehow, suddenly, a fact. An enormous, dangerous, grey old fact. We backed our trucks into a clearing in the trees, but kept our motors running and our doors open. That way, if the elephant charged, we could presumably run back to the trucks, hop in, and race away. An idiotic idea, at best. The guide was positively giddy—it was the largest and oldest elephant he had ever seen, he told us. And begged us to take a picture for him.

The elephant stood, shuffling his feet in the dust, in the middle of a narrow path in the middle of trees. His eyes were closed. He kept bobbing his trunk up and down, like someone who's fishing bobs a line in the water to attract the attention of biting fish. He seemed fairly indifferent to our creeping up on him, which is what we did, eventually. We hid in the sparse bush, crouching and breathing hard, trying to keep quiet. My husband and I took turns and after a while we even took our dusty daughter out of the truck to see him. Our Rwandan guide was there as well as our friend, who was trembling and refused to let his pregnant wife out of the truck. We furtively snapped a few photos, wincing at the sound of the shutter.

We should have stayed there for days, watching the elephant breathe and shuffle. Tossing his ears and lifting the lip of his trunk to the wind. He was beautiful, the Ancient-of-Days, and we sang his praises the whole way home.

The way home turned out to be rather elusive. Our guide for the day asked us to drop him off at his village just outside the park. We were taken to the extreme reaches of the park and out into the hills. We were anxious to make it back to Kigali before the sunset. The roads were difficult enough to navigate in the light of day, and the possibility of carjacking is always there, in Africa, after dark. At some point in our long ramble through the heights of the green hills, we thought that somehow we had become lost. We had no way to communicate this to the truck ahead of us, though, and we couldn't stop or we'd risk losing sight of them. We were flying down the roads, past mud-brick build-ings and grass huts, sometimes suddenly past a lone traveller with an enormous load on her head, or a couple of children sitting on the side of the road with their backs to the dirt track, feet dangling down the steep incline beside the path.

It was terribly hot and our truck didn't have air conditioning, so our windows had to be open to the red dust kicked up by the truck we were following. After we got home, it took days to work the dirt out of our hair and ears. When we blew our noses, we blew red. All of our clothes had red-dirt creases in them, and I still can feel my camera lens scrape inside when I focus, even today.

It came out, in the end, that we were led so far astray for honey. Our guide knew that the far-flung village we drove to "on our way home" was the best place to get it. With some of the money he made from his day with us, he bought buckets of honey.

By then we were so tired that we were husks of ourselves: emptied out into the grasslands where we had followed buffalo and giraffes, our hearts bursting from our bodies while we watched that elephant. We were full only of wild animals and wild trees. So we waited in the truck while he went to collect the honey and we studied the neatly swept dirt courtyards of the mud-brick building around us.

There were chickens and some children. Slowly a few women approached the vehicle, and some older children. Eventually we drew a large crowd that kept pushing closer to the truck, in the end pressing hands and curious faces to the windows, which we had by that time rolled a little higher. Our daughter was always a bit of a spectacle with her white-blond curly head of hair, and she had been sitting by herself in the middle of the back seat, on her knees, a little doll in a pink fuzzy sleeper beside her. By now she was so exhausted that she crawled into the front seat and lay her head down on my lap. We were surrounded, the children looked at us, bewildered, but the women laughed, covering their mouths with their hands and pointing.

We laughed a little, at ourselves, to be companionable, but soon got tired of that. Eventually our guide came back and we slowly merged out of the crowd and went on our way, careful of the chickens.

We made it home, though it was dark by the time we saw the lights of Kigali ahead. We must have parted ways with our friends and gone home to bathe, and later on we must have emailed something to our family back in Canada. I've since lost all of those long-ago emails, but the photograph of the elephant I have still. And the smell of the dust and the heat on the vinyl of the truck we lived in that one day.

What I'm missing is the wild honey. Why didn't we buy some, way up in that village in the hills? I don't think we even thought of it, then. But I think of it now, and I wish for the memory of a taste of honey, for the way home, at the top of the world in Rwanda.

A new rainy season has started. Birds have come with it. Where have they been hiding, I wonder. Deep in the forest perhaps, drinking water hidden in flower hearts and running under fallen leaves. I have been here for this season before, but the first time I didn't notice its coming.

Now I am in a new, smaller room and from the windows I can see trees turning their leaves red. This is remarkable in a country run entirely under dictatorship of green. This same type of tree, all around the city, is turning red and then letting its leaves fall. Because it is fall, my daughter says to me, matter-of-factly. Since we came to this country when she was just three, the fall season she knows is one she's learned from books and her American International playschool. I suppose it could be called that, even here—rain falls, red leaves, the birds.

The birds are trying to build a nest between the glass and the metal grill that locks up my windows at night. Every morning when we open the grill the thin long grasses the birds have brought fall in a mess on the terrace floor. I worry that they will soon leave, but it's been weeks and they haven't. Instead, two have set up house cupped deep within one of the potted plants. This seems to have encouraged the birds that still want to nest on the grill, so they persist, tirelessly building and rebuilding.

2003

A Deepening Circle

A sea turtle is a solitary creature. Who knows what sea turtles are about? Most days, not even sea turtles themselves. One night they break into the land of the living, born buried in warm sand with a hundred others. They surface on the sand and then pull themselves to the water's edge and again they go under. Around them and under them and before them are other turtles, but they don't see them, pushed on alone by their own simple need for the sea. Once water-borne they don't look back. They swim away, as far and as deep as they can go. The sea turtle goes it alone through most of life, only bumping occasionally into other sea turtles in feeding grounds (where they might mate if the timing is right), but the meetings are unremarkable, muted occasions and the sea turtle slips away as quietly as it came.

I bumped into a sea turtle myself a few weeks ago, and since then I've been reading up on them. But what a sea turtle does for most of its long life remains rather a mystery, as most of it's lived unfathomably deep.

If the sea turtle makes it down the beach and into the sea the night it hatches, it finds, as quickly as possible, a nice big patch of seaweed to hide in. If it's a large enough patch, she'll stay there for years, eating on the sly. I read somewhere that when they reach dinner-plate size the turtles will head out into the open sea, big enough to fend for themselves. How they can possibly know when they are dinner-plate size is anyone's guess (I, for one, happen to have relatively small dinner plates...), but one day she slips naked from her weedy home and opens her elegant arms to the sea. Trailing seaweed she goes, pointing her beak in a deep dive.

A male sea turtle may spend his entire life, which could last over a hundred years, swimming the seas. It is only the females who haul themselves once or twice a nesting season to beach themselves on the shore. Inexplicably, almost all of them swim back to the same beach they were hatched on. The rest of the year they may wander thousands of kilometres away, but somehow they find their way back to lay their eggs. Maybe the sea turtle can't fathom the possible existence of other shorelines after spending decades adrift. That first night spent scraping tender fins across sand makes an indelible impression, so to that same beach she must return.

One night we went looking for sea turtles. This was in February, the hottest time of the year in Gabon and the tail end of the nesting season. At about two-thirty A.M. we went walking down the white sliver of beach on a skinny finger of land pointing out into the Atlantic. The population on this peninsula is small: there's only a tiny village nearby, though you'd never know it from beachside. A few miles behind us a group of ten cabins perched on the edge of the dunes where we were staying for the weekend with friends. The night of our search was moonless, and intermittent lightning flashed silently far away over the sea. We carried flashlights but were reluctant to use them, not wanting to scare away any turtles coming up onto the shore. We headed off down the beach where earlier in the day we had seen signs of old nesting spots.

As we walked, we flicked our lights ahead and around us, illuminating the crabs that went scrambling back to the surf. We spotted two new trails leading up from the water, but the shapes we kept hopefully picking out of the darkness turned out to be logs or mounds of seaweed. Impatiently one member of our little group began to run, and we watched his light bouncing ahead of us until it disappeared. When he spotted a turtle, he came running back, breathless, to tell us she was just emerging from the water onto the beach. So two of us ran back to wake the children and two of us went on to find her again and wait for the others.

This was completely unlike any other kind of animal expedition I had so far experienced in Africa. We were without the sturdy steel walls of a vehicle or anything resembling a map. We were hunting the unknown in the dark, barefoot, unguided. It seemed to take forever to find her, we thought we had gone too far, we couldn't see anything, we tripped, we stopped, we ran for a bit, trembling. Then we saw her, or we heard her or we felt her—I don't know which came first—flipping the sand around just above the high water line, nearly among the roots of the mangrove trees that mark the forest's edge.

A leatherback sea turtle weighs more than four hundred and fifty kilograms and is meant to move in water. This was painfully obvious as we watched her struggling up the beach, thwacking her front flippers ahead of her and heaving herself forward. The track that she made looked like a single tractor tire mark, the grooves stamped deep in the sand. When she reached the tree line, she turned halfway around and dug in. She had snorted a little as she was working her way up the beach, but after that she stayed almost silent, except for the dry rasp of the sand scraped by her flipper and then thrown behind her. Between her digs she took brief pauses to rest and realign herself, moving slowly in a deepening circle.

This went on for maybe an hour, and then, after a longer pause, a more careful movement, she curved her black flipper into the shape of a cup and began scooping a deeper hole in the ground just behind her. Slowly she carved out a single tear-shaped hollow, her eyes on the sea, her back flippers moving and working, it seemed, independently, our flashlights catching the whole meticulous show.

Then came the silent laying of about fifty round, soft-shelled eggs. One flipper hovered over the hole, but we caught glimpses of the pure white, jellylike balls dropping two or three at a time on top of each other. The turtle kept still, her head still pointed to the sea, her front flippers just barely twitching. I crouched beside her and touched her side and her back, my hand tracing the thick ridges that ran from the top of her body's thick shell-that-was-not-a-shell to her tail. I softened the beam of the flashlight and shone it on her head. Her eyes blinked, wincing, a thick liquid running from them that I later read was salt being secreted through her eye glands. Both of us sat there on the sand, bewildered. Here, beside me, was an enormous sea turtle, seemingly swum from the very day God brooded over the water and created all the unthinkable things of this earth.

After she laid the eggs, the turtle pushed back the sand to cover the pit, pressing carefully down with her flipper. When the hole was concealed, she started to flip the sand more randomly back in an effort to disguise the whole event. So the ceremony came to its end and we, the congregation around her, rose to wait for the benediction, the journey back to the sea into which she would slip back as noiselessly as she had come. But all this was interrupted by a sudden storm that broke above us. We were being chased away, it seemed, having seen enough, maybe too much. If we had been sensible we would have brought our umbrellas, but in our eagerness we had come empty-handed, and our children with us.

Instantly we were soaked to the skin, and we went running wildly down the beach, scared witless by the thunder cracking and the lightning flashing around us. We ran spitting, blinking the rain from our eyes, the children hanging ragged in our arms. The flashlight's beam jogged around as we ran, and in the confusion of light the crabs on the beach lost their sense of direction. I couldn't see a thing. I stepped on one, my bare foot cracking brittle shell, and I could hear the sharp snap above even the noise of the storm.

It seemed both the end and the beginning of the world, running down that beach half blind. Like we had stepped through a crack in the surface of things and been allowed, for one night, a God's-eye view of the world. My husband had run ahead with our daughter, and when I got back to the cabin she was sitting naked on the closed lid of the toilet seat, wrapped in a towel, shivering and crying and waiting for the water in the shower to get warm.

What we missed witnessing, that night on the beach, was the return trip. I keep imagining the turtle is still there, sitting in the dark, weeping salt. No doubt she actually moved slowly back to the sea and was taken in, wordlessly welcomed home. Next year I'm going back, just to see.

On the Edge of the Primeval Forest

Madame Herrmann and Mlle. Arnoux are kind enough to hold a
short service every evening about sunset in among the smoky fires
and the seething cooking pots, and the conversation about the Bible
passages read out is often lengthy. On one occasion a native, and
one of the real savages, too, took Mlle. Arnoux to task because she
read out that no one had ever seen God. That, he said, was untrue;
he himself had once caught sight of God in the forest.

—ALBERT SCHWEITZER, *in a letter to friends*, 1924

The country of Gabon is truly, abundantly, green. It always has been.
Its story is the story of the rainforest that covers nearly eighty-five
percent of it. I live, in all possible ways, on the fringes of this story and
this country: in Libreville, its capital, situated right on the coast—you
can walk a few blocks to the sea from the middle of downtown. So I tell
the story the same way it has always been told—from the edges peering
in. No one has ever written its story from inside out. The man who saw
God in the forest has never told his story.

The earliest accounts of life in Gabon were written in the sixteenth century,
though people have lived here since Neolithic times. In the 1600s Portu-

guese traders wandered down the coast of equatorial Africa and wrote descriptions of the shorelines and the mouths of rivers. Information on the interior from the 1800s is sketchy, most of it hearsay. For the period later on in that century and into the 1900s, more documents are available, written mostly by sailors and traders, explorers and missionaries. Most of the documents are administrative reports, but there are also letters and a few travelogues, manuals for trade. It's the story of how to use the country—what to get and how to get at it. It is the same today—the number of books on trade and economics in the country far outnumbers histories or studies on its arts and culture. And, at least in English, I couldn't even get an up-to-date travel guide—the only one I found that touched on anything beyond Libreville was over ten years old.

What's fascinating about these early descriptions is that most of the writers describe Gabon, the rainforest, as a kind of green hell—a stinking, rotting, steaming, God-forsaken place. An oppressive, wretched, desolate place that swallows people whole. It devours, maims, and holds captive by any number of its curses, poisonous plants, and swarms of insects, all manner of snakes, rampaging elephants, gorillas and leopards. (Not to mention the cannibalistic natives.) The people who live here, so the writers theorize, must be desperate, eking out their survival and fighting for their lives.

The rainforest, and therefore the people who live within it and depend upon it, and therefore the country itself, is written off as pure chaos. These first impressions have stuck. In fact, I have a National Geographic on my shelf from just a few years ago that describes a section of this forest as "the last place on earth." In the article the author writes that hiking through it is "like being passed through the guts of the forest and being slowly digested." The forest is still described as a madhouse, the greenery out of hand and running rampant over the earth. The sinister primeval forest.

But what most of those writers saw were only the beginnings of the forest, the edges that rim the coast and the riverbanks of central Africa. While it's true that these areas are wild, overgrown, rambunctious bits of forest, this is because these bits have access to the sunlight at the edges. Within the rainforest, beneath the towering canopy of trees, the groundcover is sparse and walking is easy. How utterly telling that this impression still holds, and in a way this is true for so much of the continent of Africa—we see from the edges, from the shorelines and the headlines and fringes of events that catch our short attention spans. It looks wild over there, the heart of it—darkness—we imagine this still. But the green wall that runs beside the roads is impenetrable only to those who won't venture a walk inside.

The first few times we went walking in the forest, we set out with friends and our children. The kids were afraid at first and reluctant for some time to walk without the hand of a parent. But now they don't mention it. They run ahead or lag behind together, rambling along in their own way and looking mostly at the ground for the large red millipedes and long lines of ants. They shout whenever they see a particularly brilliant bug and warn everyone loudly that we must not touch it—it might be poisonous—a word they are all quite fond of repeating in very serious tones. I like to linger behind the others just for the view of these little people I know and love, travelling the rough path between the incredible stretches of trees to the sky.

The ground below us is alive and moving. Insects by the thousands if you're willing to watch, travelling under and over rotting leaves and root systems, seedpods, and fallen fruit. There are holy-high trees, the kind that are worshiped here, complete with towering buttresses—so high and wide you could make a comfortable home between them. I wonder what sort of sacred literature would have come down through the ages if there had been a written tradition in the rainforests. Epic poems in praise of trees.

Once we went into the forest with a Gabonese guide. He pointed out the many trees beside the path with wide gashes cut into the bark and sometimes whole sections of bark ripped away—to be used in traditional medicines. Sometimes a tree was so stripped it was dying, tilting back to the ground. Our guide told us proudly about his grandmother. She is blind, he said, but she knows the forest. If a child in the village is ill, she will put her hands on that child and know what he is suffering from. Then she will go into the trees and collect the right things to make medicines for that child and he will become well again.

Our guide showed us seeds and nuts and explained how they were pressed or ground or roasted. We found a few large smooth, rounded seeds; these, he told us, women wear tied round their waists when they are trying to conceive a child. We smelled the sharp-scented resin from the okoumé tree that the people collect; wrapped in leaves and grasses, it makes a candle that will burn through the whole night. He clipped a broad leaf from a plant growing in big patches between the trees and showed us how it could be used as a cup or a scoop to hold and collect water. The same leaf is used to wrap manioc or fish because it won't burn or boil but stays intact while whatever it holds inside is cooked. Manioc is still sold this way in the markets around town, and I have seen dugout canoes loaded high with neat foot-long bundles. The pygmies, our guide told us, use the leaf to waterproof their grass huts. He cut each of the children a stalk and they carried their leaves the rest of the way through the forest like flags.

Down one of the paths we spotted a group of children washing clothes in a pool of muddy water. They were kneeling beside it, scrubbing the clothes with a brush. Later we saw them wringing out a large sheet between them, a child on each end, twisting the material one way and then the other. We lost sight of them as we went further down the path, but they marched past us silently a little later, barefooted, bearing brownish loads of laundry on their heads.

"In return for very little work nature supplies the native with nearly everything that he requires for his support in his village. The forest gives him wood, bamboos, raffia leaves, and bast for the building of a hut to shelter him from the sun and rain. He has only to plant some bananas and manioc, to do a little fishing and shooting, in order to have by him all that he really needs." So wrote Albert Schweitzer while he travelled down the Ogooué River to Lamberene in 1914. Schweitzer was a brilliant scholar and medical doctor who moved to Gabon in 1913 with his wife to set up a hospital there. He lived most of the rest of his life there, on the banks of the Ogooué River. You can still visit this hospital today, see his desk and his bed and his hat and some of his books moulding away on the shelves.

Schweitzer often described the Gabonese as "the child of nature," but perhaps this is a not very accurate description. The Gabonese people have lived in the rainforest for thousands of years. This is their home; they are at home here and a part of the myriad systems that make it a whole. Their knowledge of the forest is enormous—one historian has described it as encyclopaedic—hundreds of plants and animals are used by them, and hundreds more observed and named. By outsiders, the depth and extent of this traditional knowledge is still unknown, but certainly underrated. The few existing inventories list local names and uses of plants, showing that the communities know much more about their habitats than they need to for purely practical purposes.

Fewer than a hundred years ago, the people still lived in this rain-forest in much the same way as they always had. Villages were home to about one hundred inhabitants, and each was ruled by a "big man," the head of the wealthiest, most powerful household. The forest provided food all year: there were the different seasons for various fruits, seasons to gather caterpillars, honey, mushrooms, and termites. In the dry season the village moved to camps for fishing and hunting, and year-round people collected leaves and roots, ants, larvae, snails, and crabs. The only domesticated animals kept were goats. Every year the village cut out a field from the forest and planted yams and beans, bananas, manioc. Different crops attracted different species of game, so special-ized traps were set around the fields for a steady supply of meat. Every few years the whole village shifted to a different area to cut out a new field and hunt in untapped territories.

So that was life a hundred years ago. What's happened since then is a familiar story that goes something like this: Slaves were exported from this country well into the 1900s, though the crime had been outlawed for some time by then. It was easy to hide slaves in isolated shacks along the coast for pick up. More Europeans came and set up factories, and people moved from the villages in the forest to congregate around them. Rubber was exported, as were palm oil, peanuts, and ivory. Colonial wars raged through the country, and the French burned down more villages and killed Africans by the thousands—through war and through imported diseases. Many people also died from the malnutrition that resulted from being overworked and overrun.

The French came to Gabon to make money, and they are still here today by the thousands, making money still. Gabon became officially "independent" from France in 1960. In order to develop a new Gabonese identity, the new government firebombed villages and forced people to relocate to villages that had to be situated along a main road. We've driven for whole days through these villages along the main roads. Pressed to the sides of the dirt road, they are covered in red dust; even the trees look as though they have been bronzed. Usually a river runs nearby where women are washing their clothes or their children and boys are fishing.

In every village a few old rusted oil barrels line the road and on them are placed a couple of bottles of palm wine or medicine, sometimes fruits or nuts. Often there is a stick propped up against the barrel and on it hangs something dead. We've seen monkeys and bush rats, porcupines and crocodiles, bush deer and snakes. In fact, most of the wildlife we've seen in Gabon has been dead, hanging from a stick. Sometimes what's there has been gutted and smoked—looking like the charred remains of a roadkill. Many of these animals for sale are endangered or "protected," a status which in this country, as far as I've seen, means very little if anything. Even in the capital at the only supermarket in town on Saturdays you can often buy a monkey or some sort of rare bird. In the middle of downtown someone is keeping a rare fish eagle chained to the grill of his air conditioner just outside his apartment balcony. Along a busy road in one of the quartiers a brand new sign recently went up outside a restaurant, proudly listing any number of endangered animals served up—from Gorilla and Elephant to the elusive Pangolin.

Until oil was discovered in the 1970s, the trees were the main reason for foreigners to be in this country. As the people who lived amongst those trees were pushed to the edges, the rights to thousands of hectares were granted to mostly French and, increasingly, Asian logging companies. Most of the labour is imported. The state of the camps in these areas is appalling: no running water, no medical supplies, and not enough food, which has encouraged the hunting of bush meat—illegal or not.

Logging in Gabon is highly selective. Only a few species of trees, such as the okoumé, are taken out in large quantities, but the network of roads and trails installed to reach the regions where those species grow does extensive damage to large areas. These same paths cut through the forests make for easier for bush-meat poaching as well.

The Ministry of Water and Forests in Gabon has set levels for sustainable timber production and employs agents to enforce those numbers. In 1999, on average, there was one government agent for every 86,400 hectares of logging concessions. And about one vehicle per twenty agents. So the actual amounts of lumber being logged each year is much higher than what's deemed sustainable, and every year the numbers get worse. What the Gabonese actually get from the millions of dollars worth of trees being taken out of their country each year is generally nothing more than the dust of the dangerously overloaded logging trucks that careen down the dirt roads that run beside their homes. That, and the occasional renegade log that wipes out any number of houses and every now and again, a villager or two.

I want to go back to those descriptions of the green hell, because there is something honest about them. The writers were truly overwhelmed by the forest—they were terrified of its otherness, its unknowablity. And when it is impossible for us to truly grasp the great order in it, we have no idea how it can all work together. Who could possibly even think of beginning to describe the intricate filigree that you only have to stand still to see? It sets our minds spinning out of reach. We stand astonished at the edges of our knowledge, the edges of tree roots, and tramp across leaves. Look carefully—that is a praying mantis, not a stick. At your toes is a bright red millipede as thick as your thumb and twice as long. There are hundreds of leaves on that tree, and each has a scrollwork edge you could not dream of duplicating even once in your lifetime.

The trick is not to balk and back out. Is this why we fail to protect the rainforest, why we will continue to fail it and the people who live in it? Is it essentially a failure of the imagination? Perhaps the reason why the logging companies remain reluctant to initiate sustainable production plans is because they are still looking in the old bewildered way at the wildness that is in this place. It's far too complex a problem, so they keep an eye on only a few species and tear through the rest to get them out. And get themselves out, with their lives.

Because, I suppose, the forest would take your life, if you let it. If you really wanted to understand something about it. The truth beyond that impenetrable border we see from the edges is incredible diversity, endless variation, life that is full and beautiful, growing, green. In the rainforest live species upon species, in numbers and diversity like few other places on the planet. It is not chaos but great abundance, and inside, there is enough clean green space to see it. The rainforest is one of the most elaborate and intricate systems in the world. It is not chaotic, but it is terribly complex—a state which makes it the opposite of what we deem it: vulnerable, sensitive to the most minute change. We have neither the time nor the patience today to look for the paths that pass through the rainforest, and no interest in the few people who are still travelling them.

This is still the story of Gabon and its rainforest as seen from the edges, by an outsider looking in. A long, drawn-out story that maybe means something to you and to me, much like the Bible passages read out among the cooking pots beside the river at the Schweitzer hospital meant the most to the white Western missionaries there. But in the end, the Gabonese—the only one who really belongs here—walks away into the shadows of the trees, on his way home, and we are forever left wondering if he really did catch sight of God, once, walking alone in the forest.

At a certain hour of the day the sun hits the glass in a way that makes the birds believe there are more trees beyond the windows, inside the house. Every afternoon I hear at least a few of the dull thuds that bird bodies make flying into glass. I used to cringe when I heard the sound, but so far it hasn't resulted in anything more than a bunch of bewildered-looking birds walking around on the tiled terrace floor. I've almost stopped running over to check.

These birds keep me company during the long days that I am alone since my daughter is now for the first time in school every day. But I am not entirely alone. A child, for seven months now, has taken up his own nest in the cup of my belly. I imagine his kicks might sound like the soft thud of the birds hitting glass, but they stay surprisingly silent. Like the birds, I hope he will stay quietly where he is a little while longer. One more trip across the sea before he will be born.

2003

"Fish and Fetish"

Last month, Libreville's largest daily paper, *L'Union*, ran a half-page article entitled "How to Bewitch Your Lover." It was a serious, matter-of-fact article that discussed, among other things, the fact that many women in this country are able to give birth to fish. Next to the article there was a large close-up of several of these fish: very ugly catfish-types, complete with long trailing whiskers and bulging eyes. This particular fish, when prepared by a woman and then served to her husband or lover, is supposed to ensure that the man who eats it will remain faithful to the woman who has prepared it. The article went on to describe, in some detail, how it would become almost physically impossible for that man to be unfaithful to that woman.

Of course, not every woman is lucky enough to be able to give birth to a fish. So the article also, helpfully, explains what a woman should do in this case. It advises that she catch this type of fish herself (a fairly common species which resides close to the banks of rivers and always returns to the same hole in the mud). Once in possession of such a fish, the woman is instructed to put it inside her own body for some time and hold it there, before "birthing" it herself. Then she is to immediately cook it up. If done correctly, this procedure is supposed to produce the same effect as if the hapless fellow had consumed a "naturally" birthed fish dish.

During the same month that this article ran, my own picture appeared in this newspaper—a photo of me sitting beside a child in my daughter's class, my head bent over her and she colouring a flag. The accompanying article describes how the International School has been celebrating Easter and states that I am helping a child colour the flag of Gabon. The flag of Gabon has three equal horizontal stripes: green, yellow, and blue. The flag the child is colouring is obviously not the Gabonese flag, and the child I am assisting is in fact from Zimbabwe. The school is also not celebrating Easter—it is marking International Day for which the children were to dress in their national costumes and run around all day with their country's flag tied about their necks. Obviously, some suspect reportage goes on in the pages of this newspaper.

But the fish story is not a report: it is printed under the section entitled "Women's Issues." It is more of an advice column than a story, the Ann Landers of Gabon giving romantic counsel. And there is that awful picture that I can't get out of my mind—nearly five by seven inches—of those ugly fish.

There's something up in this country, something funny going on, and everyone knows it. Gabonese are well known, respected, feared, and scorned for their persistent belief in witchcraft, or juju: their ancient traditional religions are still practised, not so secretly, in all sectors of Gabonese society, and it gets much uglier than the fish.

Some of the stories one hears around the city are, in some ways, amusing. For example, there are the stories of the midnight travellers: Gabonese who have powers that enable them to transport themselves to a different country during the night. The amusing thing is that the country these people unfailingly choose to travel to is the United States. There was a story of two boys who would go nightly *aux États-Unis dans leur petit avion*. They had a special invisible little airplane that they would fly across the Atlantic to spy on the Americans. One night they must have been having a particularly good time over there, for they forgot the time and didn't make it back to Libreville before the sun had begun to rise. Because it was becoming light, they were suspended in the air, unable to land unseen as they usually did. They decided their only option was to jump: so suddenly, out of the blue, the two boys fell from the sky. Apparently one of them broke his neck and died. But the other boy was questioned by people who had seen his fall, and that is how the story of *le petit avion* came to be known. It had to be true—after all, they had seen him fall from the empty sky.

A similar story recounts how an old man from a village in the bush could travel by night, this time on some sort of magic carpet. Once when he was walking around somewhere in the United States, the son of a family from his village recognized him. The young Gabonese gave the old man a letter and asked him to deliver it to his parents. But of course the old man could not do so for fear that his secret journeys would be discovered. Years later when the boy returned to his parents' village, he asked his parents if they had received the letter from the old man. His parents protested that the man had never left the village, and so out came the story of the magic carpet.

No one thinks it odd that these stories invariably involve the United States. We wondered why no one would ever pick another country... say France, for example, where at least they would understand the language. Someone explained it to us like this: Everyone wants to go to the States, why would they go anywhere else? Les États-Unis holds a special power over the people here. It is at once the most despised and the most revered place on earth. While everyone wants to get there, it is at the same time blamed for any number of Gabonese problems.

For example, last month there was an epidemic of eye infections around the city. One of my husband's community health workers called in sick for the day, explaining she had l'appollo. When he got off the phone he mentioned this to her supervisor who happened to be there and asked him what l'appollo was. Well, it turns out that in 1969, the year the American space mission Apollo 11 landed on the moon, there was a lunar eclipse that could be seen in Gabon, making the moon turn a reddish hue. About the same time as this lunar eclipse, there was a countrywide epidemic of conjunctivitis. So the Gabonese put the occurrences all together and came up with this: The Americans did something to the moon which caused the eclipse, which in turn caused Gabon to suffer a massive outbreak of eye infections—therefore there conjunctivitis is called l'appollo.

The same week we took our truck to a mechanic to get its air-conditioner fixed. There were two men standing around the shop, and one was complaining about how hot it had been that month. The other man said to him something like, What are you complaining about? This is Africa! The complaining man disagreed—he said it was much too hot lately, even for Gabon. He pointed to the sky and said: "C'est les Americaines, ils ont touché quelque chose en haut." (It's the Americans, they fiddled with something up there and now it's way too hot here.)

But back to fetishes: Mary Kingsley was an Englishwoman who came to Gabon in 1895. She hatd lived her entire life thus far (she was thirty-three) in England with her parents, nursing them both until their deaths, which occurred within six months of one another. Then she went to West Africa. More importantly, she went to Gabon, the country where I now live, a country which few people are even aware of. She went, she said, in search of "fish and fetish." Her father had done some studies on the fetish phenomenon and she had decided to expand on his work. And she liked to collect things like birds and toads and fishes.

I think she was also just desperate to do something and didn't much care if she got killed in the process.

She went alone, wearing her thick woollen skirts, taking her tea in the middle of the bush when necessary, travelling to remote villages where probably no white woman had ever been before. She wrote extensively about the fetish and witchcraft practices of the Bantu and the Fang. She saw elephants and gorillas and leopards in the forest. She fell into rivers and game traps. She bargained with village chiefs and traded tobacco. While reading her travelogue I could hardly believe the things she had done, where she had gone, keeping her wit and her sanity intact all the way.

In her book, *Travels in West Africa*, she devotes a large section to explaining the beliefs of the natives of this region. It's fascinating reading. Even more fascinating for me is the fact that the practices described are still around today—all around, in fact. Superstition is still very much a part of the daily thinking and daily life of people here, and is even more persistently regarded in matters of death. Kingsley's reportage on the reasoning and the ritual behind the fetish phenomenon as well as the Fang penchant for cannibalism remains one of the best firsthand sources of information on this sort of thing.

So what is going on here? Basically, the system works the same way today as it did a hundred years ago. Fetishes, or charms, are tools to whoever has them. If you have the right fetish you can do anything—from bringing someone else bad luck or illness to ensuring a successful hunt. Charms can protect a person from all the evil spirits that abound—the spirits in nature and the spirits that plague the living from the world of the dead. The fetish works when it is made up of the correct ingredients, correctly gathered, and when the right words are spoken to it, usually by a medicine man who makes it his job to know them. The desired effect can be personal or communal.

As historian linguist Jan Vansina writes in his book *Paths in the Rainforest*, traditionally fetishes were made for use against people of one's own village because of one basic vice: envy. Witches were those in the community who could kill others with their fetishes, either consciously or unconsciously. Vansina writes that this practice made sense in the context of village life because the message was constantly reinforced that each person should be careful not to invoke the envy of his neighbours; no one must stand out from the crowd. He argues that witchcraft was a notion of equality and co-operation. The village chiefs, the wealthiest men in the villages, were therefore constantly fighting off witchcraft—which must have been constantly raging against them—with scores of charms and fetishes and human sacrifices.

Death in the village was never understood to be of natural causes. When someone died, the family of that person assembled, often consulting the witchdoctor to decide who or what they could accuse of causing the death of their loved one. Often the people accused of the witchcraft were those deemed socially inferior in the village, the poor, or someone known to carry a grudge against the deceased. What followed was an ordeal by poison: the accused was forced to drink a powerful toxin; innocent persons were expected to purge themselves by vomiting, while the guilty would be unable to do so. The guilty were immediately lynched and burned, thus ridding the village of that person's evil spirit even after death.

In *Travels in West Africa*, as well as in the journals of Albert Schweitzer, who lived in Gabon for many years, this sort of thing is reported as occurring constantly in the villages. Someone is always being accused and poisoned, suspicion and fear abound. Kingsley described staying in a village hut one night and, curious as always, opening a bundle that was hanging from the ceiling. Out fell a human hand, an ear, a nose, and an eyeball or two. Schweitzer writes about the fear that gripped a village near his hospital when there was a man lurking about, looking to get himself the most powerful fetish of all—a human head.

Whatever it is that is needed for the fetish, it is most often bound in a little cloth bag, or a box, and then either carried about or hung in an appropriate spot in the home or family plantation. We once saw a sacred tree in the forest that held bundles of this sort—an old tree, its deeply rutted trunk covered with large rusted nails that looked like large tacks. The tacks ran in clusters and were overgrown with moss;

they looked like colonies of fungus on the bark. In a few places thick padlocks were attached to either the bark itself or to one of those tacks driven into the wood. In some places on the tree trunk knots of red cloth were tied to nails or little bundles were attached to metal hooks. The ground and grass around the tree was trampled down into a little clearing.

A friend came to Libreville to take over the running of an organization that aids the many refugees who enter the country; currently there are large groups of Congolese fleeing civil wars. Soon after she took over, she discovered that one of her employees was stealing large amounts of money and that many of the staff were in on the deal. She ended up firing a good many people and also eventually laying criminal charges. The one person amongst the staff who she felt had some integrity she kept on as her general secretary. This woman probably had a lot of information that her former colleagues wished to keep quiet. A few months after the changing of the guard this woman fell literally down dead, leaving small children behind. An autopsy revealed that she had been poisoned, the old Gabonese curse that still plagues the population. Our friend was careful thereafter to bring her lunches from home.

But the story continues: Last month a lost little girl wandered into the head office of this organization. She was about four years old and apparently she took to our friend immediately, walking right up to her and taking her hand. In Gabon when a lost child is discovered, the only thing to do is take him to the local TV station and get him put on a spot that runs shots of missing children. Whoever finds the child takes him home (or so it is hoped) until he is claimed. While someone was getting the vehicle to take everyone to the television station, the new general secretary took the lost child around the corner to some fruit stalls, the kind that line any available corner in Libreville, and there happened to find her mother. So no one saw the little girl again and our friend was happy to have returned the girl to her family.

A few days later, when my friend's secretary was out of the office on an errand, the rest of the staff began discussing this little lost girl incident. It turns out that most of the office believed that this little girl was actually the spirit of the poisoned secretary, coming back to visit her old boss, perhaps to get her job back. It was obvious, they told my friend, because of the way the girl had gone immediately to her and was unafraid. What's more, they said, her new secretary who had claimed to find the child's mother had actually recognized, as they did, that the child was really the dead secretary, and she had taken the child home and killed her.

This is idle, round-the-water-cooler office gossip in Gabon. Here poisonings and rumours of poisonings abound. The dead spirits that once travelled the trails through the rainforest now walk the city streets. The sacred skins of wildcats that used to hang in village huts are tacked now to the plywood boards of the shanties in Libreville. In the past, every single man and woman belonged to secret societies. Today groups meet all over the city and dance their secret dances late into the night. Next door, there is bound to be an equally ecstatic group of newly converted Christians, meeting to pray for the dancers. A friend told us about his initiation ceremony in his home village, in which he was drugged into seeing and believing impossible things that he still cannot explain—but can't deny either.

And it seems clear that the "big men," the chiefs in today's society, are still arming themselves with a battery of the most powerful charms they know to protect themselves and their influence. Whenever there is an election coming up, children go missing. Once, the beheaded body of a child was found in the trunk of a cabinet minister. A man recently told me about a family he knows whose daughter didn't come home from school one day. She was eight years old. They found her body a few days later: her eyes and nose and ears were missing, her insides torn out, and her neck twisted. A powerful official is somehow implicated in this murder, too.

The writer V.S. Naipaul reports similar stories in an essay on the Côte D'Ivoire he wrote in the 1980s. He writes about sacred ceremonies requiring human blood, of disappearing children, and the ease of buying human heads in the interior. He compares what's going on in these African countries to the sort of double life that groups of African slaves in the Caribbean once led: "There was the world of the day: that was the white world. There was the world of the night; that was the African world, of spirits and magic and the true gods." The modern world, the world of the European, the world of cities and modernity that the West has imported to these countries, is seen as an illusion. The real power of the real people of this place is held by the continuation of traditional practices. Perhaps this is the only thing that has been left them, the only thing they feel able to claim?

Or is it all about envy, still, as it was in the beginning? The wealth in this country is certainly held in the hands of an elite few. And often still the scapegoat is the powerless, the outsider, the eight-year-old Ghanaian girl.

In Gabon, three animals are traditionally regarded as perfect symbols of power. The greatest is the leopard, who hunts at night, a secretive solitary creature who hides what he kills high in the trees. The other two are the fish eagle and the python. All three are mighty hunters with little to fear themselves. These attributes are highly regarded here, where the power of survival is still a necessary preoccupation for most; perhaps it is essentially the fact of fear that carries superstition on. Fear of falling out of favour with the regime so long in power here. Fear that the oil money will dry up or that prices will fall further and send the already delicate balance of power into chaos. Fear that tomorrow a child will become ill when already there is not even enough money for meat.

Perhaps the two worlds that exist here in Gabon are in a long drawn-out competition, such as was staged in this country hundreds of years ago. Whenever two wealthy, successful families in the same village were vying for control, a competition was held to determine the chiefdom. It was up to the spirits of the forest to choose who would be successful.

All that the contestants were required to do was to perform a miracle. And the family whose tricks were deemed the most miraculous—they were given the village.

We return "home" to Gabon again, two years after we first arrived. Here we go again, into a new life, bursting into what seems a watery world. We are underground here, under water, thick air, and heat. The tropical haze that hangs here embraces us immediately.

This time we are four—we've brought our six-week-old baby boy. He thinks, so far, that Gabon is too bright; he's bedazzled. He shuts down into sleep when we've been out in the heat for too long. He adores the banana tree's turning, knock-about leaves. I realize, as I begin to write again, how my sentences are now bound to fragment even more. The baby wakes. The sentence full stops.

We spend the first few days wreaking mass carnage on the ants that have taken over our bedroom and kitchen. I leave little bubbles of arsenic in their path several times a day and they come in a rush to eat it. In the morning we wake up to piles of dead ants lying around the perimeter of the room. The ones in the kitchen disappeared after one dose. No doubt they're lying in the back of some cupboard, waiting to be discovered when we go.

Giant black ants had taken up residence in the walls and roof of our bathroom. When I discovered them, there were at least fifty milling about on the tile floor and more dropping from the ceiling around the light fixture. These ants are so large you can hear them hit the ground and hear them run madly inside the ceiling when my husband comes home and sends poisonous blasts through the hole in the roof that they've made. It takes a few doses to get rid of them; we see them exit the building by the hundreds via a crack in the outside wall. After a few weeks of this, we've successfully reclaimed our territory.

The birds that built their nest in the potted tree on the terrace while I was pregnant are back. Or some relative of theirs. Building more nests. Dropping weedy gifts through the window grate and into flowerpots. I'm glad to see them. Before we left our daughter was lifted up to peer into the nests and see their tiny eggs. Now, a few days after we've arrived, we find a baby bird sitting in a heap underneath a potted yucca. My husband goes out to inspect. It seems it must be just learning to fly—my husband scoops it up, and only then does it try to get away. Susanna runs outside and she is able to hold the baby bird in the cup of her two hands for a few moments before it flops out and away.

2004

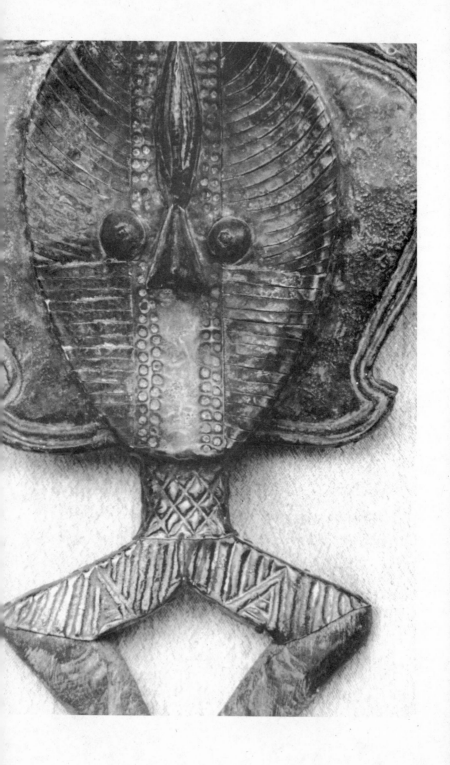

A Necessary Silence

The Fang people were once wanderers. They travelled from northeast Africa for centuries, itinerant souls. By the mid to late nineteenth century groups of them had settled themselves down in Cameroon and Gabon, and their descendants live here today, still. And for a while I'm wandering here among them.

Accompanying them on their journeys were the bones of their most esteemed ancestors, carried in boxes or cylindrical containers made of bark—skulls of very wealthy men, for example, and the spines of especially fertile women. The long leg bones of infamous warriors and the fragile finger bones of the best artists and craftsmen. The more bones a bundle held, the more powerful it was believed to be. An anonymous figure of wood or copper perched on top of these containers to protect them and to mark them as sacred vessels.

It was not only the Fang that carried such bundles to hold their dead. Around them in small communities scattered throughout the dense rainforests were more than forty ethnic groups that made similar reliquaries of their venerable ancestors. When these communities moved around they took their bones along with them—transportable shrines.

I imagine this ritual starting with one old man who, when he felt he was dying, begged his family not to bury him when it was all over, but to carry him on. Loathe to be left alone, he argued that his bones were accustomed to being in motion, he was afraid to be left in the sedentary silences of the grave.

But perhaps they took the bones along just for the company. The reassurance of the remains of those who had travelled the forest paths before them, dug the same earth, gutted the same fish. And better to remember those who had walked the same paths with some success. Imagine the silence of a small group of humans wearing down a path through the trees or living on a beaten-down island in the rainforest, the sea of green around them, the enormous breaths of the tree giants and the myriad eyes of the animals and insects. They were vastly outnumbered. So they kept the dry knocking bones of the dead for company.

I am in this place now, living here, mostly alone. Swept up, isolated. My island in this rainforest-city has been my desk in a small room of tile and cement. Around me is the sea of citizens of an almost other world, speaking their languages and negotiating their ways around me, regardless of me and sometimes in spite of me. Whose bones have I for company?

When consulting the ancestors, the various peoples of Gabon would dress up the figures or heads that sat on top of the bone-bundles. They were adorned with feathers and fancy collars and taken out of the carefully constructed shelters where they were kept most of the time, together with the bone boxes of other village families. They were set up to watch the sacrifice of animals and to be anointed with the freshly spilled blood. Sometimes the people took the figures and danced them about in a makeshift theatre. Spectacles to mark the unspeakable mysteries of life, to respect and remember the dead. Their spirits were thought at these times to grace the village with their presence, and then the village could hope to be safe, to be united, to be fed.

I carry no bones. But what have I brought on this journey from my own ancestors, if anything? Fragile photographs are the most tangible reliquaries I have. I wonder what lurks in my blood, in my own bundle of bones—my body. What inherited diseases, passions, ideas. I wonder if I have inadvertently followed in some of my ancestors' wandering ways. My grandparents on both sides of my family were immigrants. They moved from the Netherlands to Canada in the 1950s, a long journey that would end in permanent residence. They wondered if they would see their families or "the old country" again. They took baby sheets and silver. But my grandmother also carried the just-begun bones of my mother in her belly, rocking her unknowingly through the long days at sea.

Perhaps we Westerners are more apt to hold on to the things of the dead. Heirlooms that have been fingered and polished and later left to children. And those old photographs, fraying at the edges and pressed carefully into books. Common names run through family lines like a refrain—perhaps they mark memories or hold some antique reverence.

I will give the baby I have carried in my own blood-bundle across the seas a name to echo across our various times and places. And he will sleep with his head on the sheets his great-grandmother embroidered when she was a teenager in Holland. Perhaps she was daydreaming already then of the long journey. I imagine my child will dream of the opposite. His own little body will have flown a ridiculous amount of times across the world already, by then—so he will dream only of rest.

The statues that sat atop the bone bundles were often stylized heads of wood with long slender necks. Or they were flat shovel-shaped heads covered in copper or brass strips. They had long necks or supportive stands that enabled them to be placed securely into the bone bundle, which acted as a torso. They were not meant to represent a certain person but to act as guards, as warnings. The eyes, often large, were made of round metal, and the noses resembled sharp, long, thin pyramids. The ears curved on level with arching foreheads, and most of the faces were missing mouths or the mouth was reduced to a narrow slit stretched across the long pointed chin. The mouth disappears, drawn down to nothing, silent under the eyes and the imposing brow.

I have one of these reliquary sculptures on my desk. I think of it as a she—it looks like the head of a girl to me, but I know the shape of her hair is thought to represent the headdresses of ancient warriors. Her eyes are brass tacks. Her hair starts at the top of her head, falling back and revealing a huge forehead which reflects the light from my window. She is dark brown and her ears are small, the bottoms of them parallel to her eyes. Around the right ear are small holes made by tunnelling insects. Her nose is thin and long, the bottom a bit scuffed. Beneath her nose the wood curves out to form a narrow ledge, its outer edge a thin line of a mouth shorter than the space between her eyes. She has a long neck covered with woven strips of bark.

I want to take this figure as totem. She is all bright eyes and silence. I want to be that in the world—watching; I want to be awake like she is, always alert but contemplative, quiet. She faces head-on all the beauties, sorrows, mysteries of this place. I can't decide if being a writer is compatible with this; it seems sometimes the opposite. But no, this eyes-wide-open witnessing is how it all begins. Words both the perfect reliquary head for the bones of the dead and the right place for laying down warm blood. Words as warnings and words as memory. Words to keep the lonely wandering ones company on the way.

There is a necessary silence to keep when you are roaming a foreign land. And, except for writing, I've tried to keep it. I wanted the silence for company, so I made few friends. I wanted the peace of anonymity, the blur of an unlearned language around me as insulation. Something presses; meaning presses its wild wing behind my eyes. But I have no names yet. And my sojourn here is brief.

For my journey home I'll take this reliquary head that now sits on my desk, but the bones I will leave behind. They weren't a part of the original purchase anyway, and I hope they are at rest somewhere in the trees or bundled up tight with some other old ones. The silence of this dark head of wood will speak to me of this place when I am gone.

They're still here, those birds. They're some sort of finch, my botanist friend tells me. Small, black and white. Now four months old, my son sits up on my lap and watches them flit. They hop back and forth from potted plant to window grate and sometimes they fly up to the wires lining the street below. I throw out my breadcrumbs to them after lunch. I hope the new renters will keep some of the plants so the birds will stay after we've gone.

I've pinched the dried-up old nest from the red leaves of the tree they originally nested in. It will fly home with me to Canada and I'll keep it for my son. It will be a mysterious souvenir of the place he was made in, but not born into. Where he stayed the first half-year of his life but will never remember. Somehow the nest may keep it real, the signals from place to place that we carry with us in our bodies, even from the once-homes we will never return to.

More likely, it will be confiscated at customs when we land in Canada, or it will disintegrate into so much yellow dust in the dry Alberta air. But it's the thought that counts. And there are hours of them, wrapped tight within that messy ball of long grasses that I will carry home.

2004

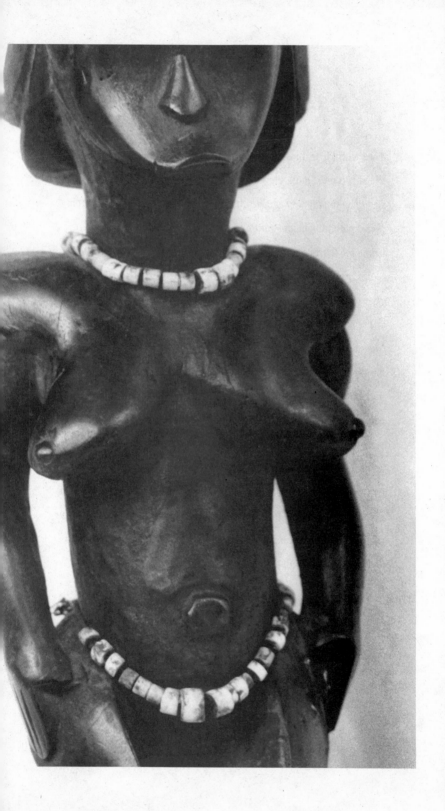

Migration

I went looking for the words to end this journey, I wanted the words for return. But there is no way home, no way to get back to where we came from. I realize this now that we are back in Canada, for four months already, the longest period of time we've spent here in the past three years. Relationships have yearlong holes in their tenuous fabrics. Our families have carried on without us. We've missed out on the various *Idol* TV shows, movies, and phenomena such as Botox, so our social skills are somewhat lacking. We are welcomed, in many ways, but we are held more carefully than we were before we left. This makes sense, for there is an uncertainty in our embrace. Once upon a time we rejected this place and left these people, and for that there will always be questions.

We have bought ourselves a house with an overgrown and dying garden. Our daughter enjoys fall for the first time she can remember, and collects ladybugs. She likes to tell people that we used to have banana trees in our back yard and that once our guard ate an enormous lizard. But no one here understands what a guard is, and she has a difficult time explaining. It is one of the unquestionable concepts she has learned about the world, something she simply knows without reason, the same as a child who has grown up in the West understands that red means stop and green, go.

Somewhere deep in my body I feel the need to fly. Or flee. Does a body get used to the flights, as the mind most certainly does? But it's not really true, I don't want to go back, I want this—this settling. But because I need to articulate this, because I want to write the false ending to my journey, I know it's still a struggle.

So I can't write the return. It wouldn't be entirely true, it's not possible. I've become a migrant, a refugee, a dweller in uncertain times. Time and place have turned fluid and I've become, of necessity, a swimmer. Part mythical mermaid, and I wonder how long my fish parts must be out of water to become strong enough to stand on this dry land.

There is a distance the soul never loses sight of, once it has seen. This shifts my perspective, it has skewed my thinking, and this must explain the silences my family and friends notice. You seem distant, is the common complaint. I feel distant. I am still away. To return is to lie about the past.

In Gabon, there is a religious group called Bwiti who make long journeys into the world of spirits. They return to their lives with new names. The initiation ceremony is very beautiful. It involves midnight processions into the jungle with candles to find the saplings of certain trees. Antelope horns are blown to announce to the ancestors the coming of a questing spirit. The initiate is watched over by an appointed father and mother who lead her down to the river at midday to hear her confession of sins. They rub her down with flowers and leaves and powdered bark from the trees around them. "Learn these trees," they tell her, for Bwiti is the religion of trees, the religion of the great green far-reaching forest. Some of these leaves have strong scents, perfumes to attract the dead and to incite their pity on the one who is coming to call.

The initiate crawls through the legs of her Bwiti father and mother. She is washed and dressed in a white robe and struck on the head with flowers so that her skull may open like an infant's to allow her soul to escape. The director of the ceremony lights a small block of pitch and places it on a manioc leaf to float downstream through her legs. The "soul boat" floats down the river to the sea, along the same path the initiate's soul will take when wending its way to the ancestors.

The initiate takes heaps and heaps of drugs to enable this journey. The drug is *eboga*, found in the root bark of the *eboga* bush which is rasped into fine powder and eaten directly or diffused in water and then drunk. This is the same root that the colonialists allowed the locals to eat while they built the railway in these areas, because it suppresses fatigue. It is eaten in Gabon today to allow the adherents of Bwiti to dance through their nightlong ceremonies. Once or twice in a lifetime it is taken, in an initiation ceremony like this one, in huge quantities, leaving the initiate in a near comatose state. In fact, only when the initiate literally falls to the ground in a stupor is the ceremony deemed a success. The soul has obviously abandoned the body at this point and begun its crossing to the land of the dead.

Many Bwiti embark on this arduous journey with pressing questions for their ancestors. They want the advice of the dead on this messy business of life. But mostly they simply want to see something. That is what they say, when asked. They want the chance to see beyond their lives.

In the visions the adherents of Bwiti describe, there is almost always a long path through the forest. The path is red or black, and often presents some sort of obstacle that must be overcome before they can continue. But there is always the forest. Life and death are both through the endless paths in the forest. Only in their visions, though, can they fly as they travel down the long path.

In his book, *Bwiti: An Ethnography of the Religious Imagination in Africa*, James W. Fernandez writes that eating *eboga* represents both the forest itself and power over the forest. He says that in the midst of all the pressure for the people to leave their villages for the cities and paid labour, *eboga* returns them to their forest. The Bwiti eat the forest. But they also overcome it.

When initiates return from the land of the dead they often adopt new names, to represent their new life. They feel they have new strength and energy, new purpose in their lives. For who would not be stronger after a journey to the dead? They have returned, they have lived through it, they have tasted death but in the end they have spit it out and taken the red road home.

There is a greeting in Gabon, mbolo, which an early missionary to Gabon translated as a wish that the person addressed should be free from the threat of death. It seems fitting to me that the one large grocery store in Libreville, the capital, should be called Mbolo. In fact, now that I think about it, in my first visit to the store I did feel rather blessed—we had come from Rwanda where such *supermarchés* didn't exist.

The Bwiti say,

> I come to a new country which is the cemetery. I strike out with the raffia streamers. Lightning and thunder. Sun and Moon, Sky and Earth. They are twins together. They are life and death. They are twins together. The yawning hole of the grave and the new life, they are twins together. [1]

Death is so ordinary an event in Gabon that no one looks away, no one covers the corpse. Death is regarded as indifferently as the many unplanned, accidental births. And now I see the relationship between all the children running unheeded through the slums and the anonymous, unclaimed dead—they are inseparable, insufferable twins, death and life.

There are so many children missing fathers, and often their "mothers" are their grandmothers, aunts, or older sisters—whoever is hanging around that day. The date of birth on their *actes de naissance* is often wrong, their names misspelled on their identification papers, their actual age questionable. No one bothers to get it right in the first place, and no one bothers to correct it later on because it costs money and sometimes days of waiting in long lines for the enormously apathetic administrators. When my husband walked through the streets, sometimes he would hear someone shouting at a child—hey, there goes your father. And children would run after him, for they could see or they had been told that they were half-white, and here was a white man coming, maybe for them. Who claims these children? Life does, I suppose, and takes them on this first journey, until later down the road, under cover of wild and terrible trees, they meet the other.

Once, on the main road in Libreville that runs beside the ocean and through the downtown, a dead man lay. He was there for about thirty hours, all day in the sun and through the night. His eyes were open wide and his arms stretched out over his head. Part of his head was smashed in and he was nearly naked. My five-year-old daughter would have passed only inches away from his body as she was driven to kindergarten that day, as he was lying right where we needed to turn onto the road. But this morning my husband had cut across the median just before the turn-off because we were running late and he could see that the traffic was jammed—the cars were moving slowly as they avoided hitting the body in the right-hand lane. No one, including the police, would pick him up, because no one knew who he was and because no one wanted to be saddled with the cost of burying the anonymous dead. I didn't hear what happened to him; he merely disappeared. Earlier in the year it was a young girl who washed up on the beach that they carried to put on display in the middle of the road, right in front of the Intercontinental Hotel.

Joy, joy, the ancestors give joyful welcome and hear the news. The troubled life of the born ones is finished, finished, finished. And now the disciplines of the dead. I go to the dead. All the misfortunes are shorn away! They leave, they leave. They leave. They leave. Everything clean, clean. All is new, new. All is bright, bright. I have seen the dead and I do not fear. [2]

I have seen the dead here, I have travelled the red road through the forests and the town, but I am not a Bwiti believer, I cannot dance all night, I still feel fear. I feel my head has been broken, as was the initiate's; my soul has escaped and journeyed, but I return to my life without a new name.

I have hung the masks of Gabon on my Canadian walls. These masks are said to represent the dead, the ancestors. When the faces of the dead are donned in Africa, it is believed that the ancestors come down to judge and to visit the living. Mine are old masks—and now their power is ceremonial, representative, like the power of the Queen in Canada. Here on my grey walls they are husks of themselves. Beautiful and strong though, still.

The ancient Hebrews thought about the past as before them, not behind them as we think of it. Their logic was simple: We can see what has happened in the past. It is the future that is unknown, we cannot see it, it hides behind us. I suppose the various Gabonese tribes have this same sense—it is what has passed that guides us. The dead are still twinned to life, and those who are lost here are still there, ahead of us.

My past lies before me, then, and not behind, even if it encroaches somewhat on the view from here. That way I can keep an eye on where I have been and what I have seen, and what has passed will guide me. What comes next is always unknown. *Everything clean, clean. All is new, new. All is bright, bright.* I strike out with raffia streamers.

Acknowledgements

I owe a great deal of thanks and love to my parents Roy and Susan Schouten for their constant encouragement and tireless love. I'm grateful for others who have been generous and helpful in different ways, some of you as supportive family members, some as readers of my earliest drafts, but all of you excellent and very dear friends: Jennifer Berkenbosch, Theresa Brandsma, Jerome and EllaMae Cupido, Lee Elliot, Suzanne Knol, Wenda Salomons, Päivi Salonen, Sarah Schouten, Amy Vankeeken and James Vriend. Much love and thanks to my grandparents Wilfred and Ann Vandermeer.

Many thanks to Elisabeth Harvor and to Greg Hollingshead for their patience, generosity, and excellent advice while working with me on some of these essays. Thanks to Jill Fallis for her careful and kind editing, and Wendy Johnson for the creation of the map.

I would also like to thank the Alberta Foundation for the Arts for an individual project grant and the Banff Centre for the Arts for access to their Individual Artist Residency/Leighton Studio Program.

Sincere thanks to everyone at the U of A Press for their exceptional care in the making of this book. And special thanks to Wenda Salomons for the gift of her fine photography.

A thousand thanks to Shawna Lemay whose support, enthusiasm, and friendship has made all the difference. I could not (or would not) have done it without you.

All love and thanks to Doug and to Susanna (and now to Reuben too). You three are the very best of companions, for any journey.

Notes

The VolcanoO1. Annie Dillard, "The Volcano," *Ploughshares* 49 (1989): 11.

Swallow the Black Seeds

1. Simone Weil, *The Simone Weil Reader* (Wakefield, RI: Moyer Bell, 1999), 332.

Migration

1. James W. Fernandez, *Bwiti: An Ethnography of the Religious Imagination in Africa* (Princeton: Princeton University Press, 1982), 488.
2. Ibid.

Readings

Fernandez, James W. *Bwiti: An Ethnography of the Religious Imagination in Africa.* Princeton: Princeton University Press, 1982.

Gourevitch, Philip. *We Wish to Inform you that Tomorrow we will be Killed with our Families.* Vancouver: Douglas and McIntyre, 1998.

Kingsley, Mary. *Travels in West Africa.* London: Phoenix Press, 2000.

Lilburn, Tim. *Living in the World as if it were Home.* Dunvegan, ON: Cormorant Books, 1999.

Naipaul, V.S. *The Writer and the World.* Toronto: Alfred A. Knopf, 2002.

Schweitzer, Albert. *The Primeval Forest.* Baltimore: John Hopkins University Press, 1998.

Vansina, Jan. *Paths in the Rainforests: Toward a History of Political Tradition in Equatorial Africa.* Madison: University of Wisconsin Press, 1990.

Weil, Simone. *The Simone Weil Reader.* Edited by George A. Panichas. Wakefield, RI: Moyer Bell, 1999.

List of Photographs

* *photographs by Wenda Salomons*
   (art and artifacts from the author's collection)
† *photograph by D. Woudstra*
   All other photographs by A.S. Woudstra.